Heavenly Hash Celestial Delights

A Collection of 50 Out of this World Cookbook Recipes

Sherry A. Martinez

Paperback ISBN: 978-0-61526-847-7
eBook ISBN: 978-1-7340874-1-3

Half and Half is a registered trademark of Land O'Lakes, Inc
Cool Whip and Jell-O are registered trademarks of Kraft Foods Group Brand LLC
Canada Dry Ginger Ale is a registered trademark of Canada Dry Ginger Ale, Inc
7-Up, Sprite are registered trademarks of Dr. Pepper Snapple Group

Food Photography by Sherry A. Martinez
Cover and Interior Design by Ghislain Viau

Dedicated to my grandmother, "Addie", a wonderful cook and baker and my Astronomer Raul, who is always looking up at the heavens.

Contents

Foreword

This cookbook combines two of my favorite activities, Astronomy and cooking. I hope it inspires many cooking and baking adventures, especially with the young, and leads to a fun way to explore and discuss a little bit about celestial objects, the Solar System, great galaxies and stars, famous astronomers and observatories along the way.

The cookbook consists of 50 recipes divided into five sections with individual recipes astronomically titled. Some of the recipes are remembered treasures, newly updated and retitled, from cooking with my grandmother Addie and her well worn, much written in cookbooks. The recipes are truly archival in nature dating from the 1920s, Depression era 1930s and World War II and provide a fascinating look into life in rural America during those times. The recipe for her famous long johns, now whimsically titled "Lunar Long Johns" is included. Another recipe, "Asteroid Belt Rock Candy" comes from my 6th grade science class. Some of the recipes have been passed along by friends and relatives and reflect a spice or "secret" ingredient added by the author. Yet others are recipes of my own design.

All of the recipes have been used many times in various meals, snacks and drinks before, during or after visits to observatories, nights of celestial viewing or daytime solar observing.

Happy Sunspots and Bon Appetit!

Astro-gastronomically yours—

Sherry A. Martinez

In the Beginning...

Big Bang Brownies

The Big Bang is a theory supported by many astronomers and scientists about how the Universe was created from a single point of energy about 13.8 billion years ago and expanded to include the stars, galaxies and celestial objects we see today.

Ingredients

- ▶ 3 Eggs
- ▶ 1¾ Cups Sugar
- ▶ 1½ Cups Flour
- ▶ 1 Cup Chocolate Chips
- ▶ 1 Cup Multicolored Sprinkles
- ▶ 1 Cup Vegetable Oil
- ▶ ¾ Cup Cocoa
- ▶ 2 Teaspoons Vanilla Extract
- ▶ ½ Teaspoon Salt

Directions

Combine all ingredients in a large bowl, adding chocolate chips last. Pour into an ungreased 9 x 13 inch pan. Preheat oven to 350 degrees Fahrenheit. Bake mixture at 350 degrees Fahrenheit for 30 minutes or until toothpick inserted into brownies comes out cleanly. Let cool, then frost with favorite frosting, mixing in the sprinkles for a fun effect. Perhaps the expansion of the Big Bang looked like something similar. Enjoy.
Servings: About 24 Big Bang Brownies.

Around the Solar System...

Sun Tea

The Sun at the center of our Solar System is a yellow dwarf star, with a surface temperature of around 5700 degrees Celsius. The Sun powers the Solar System.

Ingredients

- ▶ 5-6 Peach or Lemon teabags
- ▶ 1 additional flavored teabag of your choice
- ▶ 1 Gallon glass container

Directions

Place 5-6 peach or lemon flavored teabags, along with an additional flavored teabag of your choice into a 1 gallon glass container. Add cold water to almost the top of the container and cover. Place where sunlight strikes the container directly outside for 4-6 hours. After tea has reached the desired taste and golden brown hue, remove from sunlight and remove the assorted teabags. Add honey or sugar if desired for taste. Refrigerate tea and use within 2 days. Sun tea is best served over ice. For extra zest add a sprig of mint or slice of lemon to individual glasses of tea. Enjoy!

Sunspot Cookies

Sunspots are dark spots on the Sun's surface. Sunspots appear darker because they are colder then the regions around them. The number of sunspots increases and decreases over an 11 year cycle. Never look directly at the Sun.

Ingredients

▶ 1 Cup Butter
▶ 1 Cup Powdered Sugar
▶ ⅛ Teaspoon Salt
▶ 1 Teaspoon Vanilla
▶ 2 Cups Flour
▶ 1 Cup Finely Chopped Walnuts or Almonds

Equipment

♦ Hand Mixer

Directions

Preheat oven to 350 degrees Fahrenheit. Mix butter, ½ cup powdered sugar and vanilla in large bowl with electric hand mixer on medium speed until light and fluffy. Add flour, walnuts or almonds, mixing on low speed until well blended. Dough will be lumpy due to adding the walnuts or almonds (the sunspots). Shape into 1 inch balls and place 1½ inches apart on nonstick baking sheet. Bake approximately 18 minutes. Roll warm cookies in ½ cup of powdered sugar until evenly coated (optional), then cool. *Servings: About 18 sunspots.*

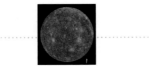

Mercury Minestrone Soup

Mercury is the closest planet to the Sun. It is also the smallest planet in the Solar System and is named for the Roman winged messenger of the gods, Mercury.

Ingredients

- ▶ 4 Cups Water or Vegetable Stock
- ▶ 1 Can Northern Great Beans, drained
  (other types of white beans can be substituted)
- ▶ 3 Stalks Celery, diced
- ▶ 1-2 Onions, sliced
- ▶ 3 Carrots, sliced
- ▶ 1 Potato, cubed
- ▶ ½ Head of Cabbage, shredded or chopped
- ▶ ½ Teaspoon Garlic, minced
- ▶ 1 Teaspoon Rosemary
- ▶ 1 Teaspoon Oregano
- ▶ 1 Tablespoon Parley
- ▶ 1 Cup Pasta, cooked

Directions

In a large pot, mix together water or vegetable stock, celery, onions, cabbage, carrots, oregano, parsley, potato and rosemary. Simmer 45-60 minutes, then add pasta. Cook on low heat until pasta is tender, adding more liquid if needed. Add beans and cook an additional 3-4 minutes. *Servings: 7-8 Cups of soup.*

Venus Valentine Cookies

Venus is the second planet from the Sun, named for the Roman goddess of love and beauty. It is shrouded in clouds and is the hottest of the planets at 864 degrees Fahrenheit.

Ingredients

- ▶ 6 Cups Flour
- ▶ 2 Cups Butter
- ▶ 2 Cups Sugar
- ▶ 2 Eggs
- ▶ 2 Teaspoons Vanilla or Almond Extract
- ▶ 3 Teaspoons Baking Powder
- ▶ 1 Teaspoon Salt

Directions

Cream butter and sugar until light and fluffy, then add eggs and vanilla or almond extract to the mixture and mix well. Mix dry ingredients slowly into the butter mixture, mixing until flour is completely blended in. Chill for 2 hours, and then roll mixture to desired thickness and cut with heart shaped cookie cutter. Bake on ungreased or no stick baking sheet at 350 degrees Fahrenheit for about 8-10 minutes or until golden brown around the edges. *Servings: About 3 dozen Venus Valentine cookies.*

Earthly Egg Salad Sandwiches

Direct to you from the 3rd planet from the Sun, Earth!

Ingredients

- ▶ 1 Egg
- ▶ 2 Egg Whites
- ▶ 2 Tablespoons Nonfat Mayonnaise
- ▶ 1 Tablespoon Sweet Pickle Relish or Gherkin pickles finely chopped
- ▶ 1 Teaspoon Dijon Mustard
- ▶ ½ Cup Alfalfa Sprouts (optional)
- ▶ Salt and Pepper
- ▶ 2 Slices Bread or toast
- ▶ 1 Cup Mulitcolored Sprinkles

Directions

Blend egg and egg whites in a bowl. Cook the egg mixture in a nonstick frying pan the way you prefer them, then remove from pan and let cool for a few minutes. Cut or mash the eggs, blending mayonnaise, mustard, sweet pickle relish or chopped gherkin pickles with the eggs. Add salt and pepper to taste and spread the egg salad onto a slice of bread or toast. Add alfalfa sprouts if desired and cover with the other slice of bread or toast and enjoy! *Servings: 1-2 egg salad sandwiches.*

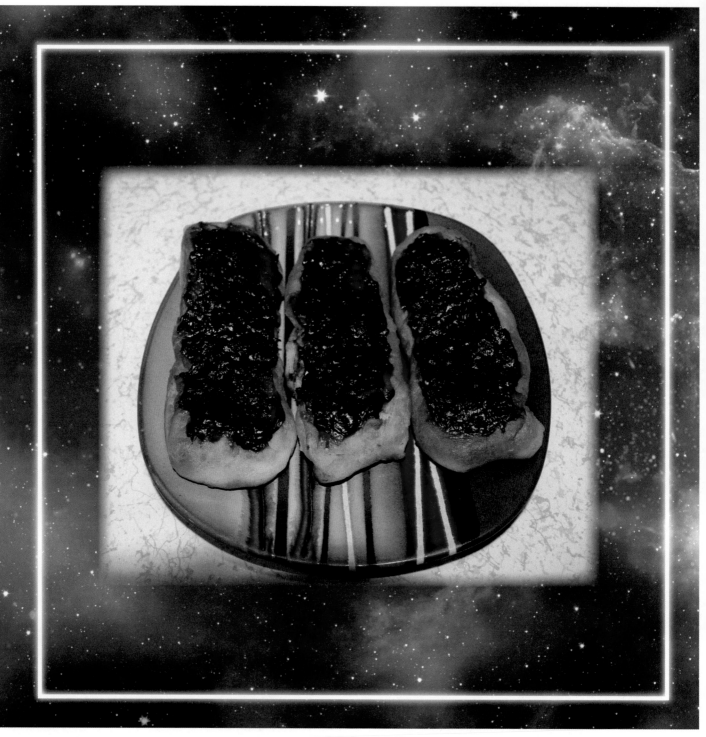

Lunar Long Johns

The Moon is Earth's only satellite. It is 1/4th the size of Earth, filled with craters and impacts, and orbits the Earth approximately every 27.3 days. When looking at the moon some people see a face, often called the "Man in the Moon", while others see a rabbit or a girl holding a mirror... What do you see?

Ingredients

- ▶ 1 Cup Evaporated Milk
- ▶ 2 Eggs
- ▶ 2 Packages Dry Yeast
- ▶ 3½ Cups Flour
- ▶ ½ Cup Shortening
- ▶ 1 Tablespoon Sugar
- ▶ 1 Teaspoon Salt
- ▶ ½ Teaspoon Vanilla Extract
- ▶ ½ Teaspoon Nutmeg
- ▶ Frying Oil

Equipment

- ◆ Frying Pan or deep fat fryer skillet
- ◆ Candy thermometer

Directions

Mix shortening, evaporated milk, vanilla extract, eggs, sugar, salt and flour together in a bowl. Dissolve yeast into ½ cup warm water in another bowl. Use candy thermometer to test for 110 to 115 degrees for best results with the yeast. Let stand for 2-3 minutes. Add nutmeg to the yeast mixture, then add both to the first mixture. Add flour to create a soft dough to work with. Knead dough for 7-8 minutes, then cover with a clean cloth and wait for the dough to rise, about 1 hour. Punch the dough down, recover with the cloth and wait about 45 minutes for dough to rise again, then uncover. Roll the dough out onto a floured surface and cut into 4-5 inch lengths by 1 inch widths. Place on ungreased baking sheet and wait for the strips to double in size, approximately 45 minutes. Pour 3 or 4 inches of frying oil in pan or skillet, heating to 375 degrees Fahrenheit, (check with the Candy thermometer), then lower the strips one or two at a time into the oil and fry until light brown on both sides, about 2 minutes per side. Remove from oil, and drain on paper towels. Let cool then frost with glaze or frosting of your choice. *Servings: About 18 Lunar Long Johns.*

Glaze

A popular old time long john glaze consists of boiling ¼ cup butter and 2 tablespoons evaporated milk for 3-4 minutes, adding your favorite flavoring (optional) and confectioner's sugar to thicken.

Moondrops

The Moon has virtually no atmosphere, and much less gravity than Earth. Objects weigh about 1/6th of what they would on Earth. On July 20, 1969 Neil Armstrong became the first person to step on the moon, uttering these famous words "One small step for man, one giant leap for mankind".

Ingredients

- ▶ 1½ Cups Flour
- ▶ 1 Egg
- ▶ ½ Cup Creamy Peanut Butter
- ▶ ½ Cup Butter
- ▶ ½ Cup Sugar
- ▶ ½ Cup Packed Brown Sugar
- ▶ 1 Teaspoon Baking Powder
- ▶ ¾ Teaspoon Baking Soda
- ▶ ¼ Teaspoon Salt
- ▶ Package of chocolate chips or pieces

Directions

Preheat oven to 375 degrees Fahrenheit. Mix butter, creamy peanut butter, sugar, brown sugar and egg in a bowl. Add flour, baking powder, baking soda and salt to the original mixture, combining until a sticky dough forms. Roll into little balls and place on a greased cookie sheet, then bake 8-10 minutes until moondrops are golden brown. Remove and place chocolate chips or pieces in center of each moondrop while warm.
Servings: 18 moondrops.

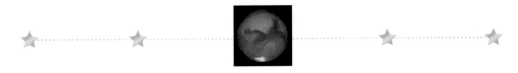

Martian Meatloaf

Fourth planet from the Sun Mars is often called the "Red" planet due to iron oxide deposits in the soil. Mars has the largest canyon in the Solar System measuring over 2500 miles.

Ingredients

- ▶ 2 Pounds Ground Beef or Pork
- ▶ 2 Eggs, slightly beaten
- ▶ 1 Cup Onion, chopped
- ▶ ⅓ Cup Parsley Leaves, minced
- ▶ ¼ Cup Golden Raisins
- ▶ ⅔ Cup Barbeque Sauce of your choice
- ▶ 1 Celery Stalk, chopped fine
- ▶ 1 Carrot, chopped fine
- ▶ 1 Cup Bread Crumbs
- ▶ 2 Tablespoons unsalted butter
- ▶ 2 Teaspoons Salt
- ▶ 2 Teaspoons Worchestershire Sauce
- ▶ 1½ Teaspoons Ground Pepper

Directions

Preheat oven to 350 degrees Fahrenheit. In a large fry pan or skillet cook onion, celery and carrot in the butter, over medium heat, for about 5 minutes. Cover skillet and cook until carrots are soft. Stir in salt and pepper, Worchestershire sauce and ⅓ cup of barbeque sauce. Mix together with meat, eggs, cooked vegetables, bread crumbs, golden raisins and parsley leaves in a bowl, then form into a loaf and place in pan. Brush meatloaf with the remaining barbeque sauce and bake in the oven for 60 minutes. *Servings: About 14-15 portions.*

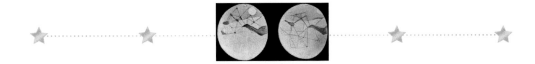

Lowell Canal Cannolis

Astronomer Percival Lowell (1855-1916) of the famed Lowell Observatory in Flagstaff, Arizona sketched "canals" which he thought supported life on Mars.

Ingredients

- ▶ 12 Homemade or Pre-packaged Cannoli Shells
- ▶ 2 Pounds Ricotta Cheese, well drained
- ▶ 1½ Cups Confectioner's Sugar
- ▶ 2 Ounces Mini Chocolate Chips
- ▶ 1 Teaspoon Vanilla or Almond Extract
- ▶ ½ Teaspoon Ground Cinnamon or Nutmeg

Directions

Place ricotta cheese in a bowl. Add confectioner's sugar to the ricotta cheese and mix until fully blended. Add the vanilla or almond extract, along with the ground cinnamon or nutmeg to the sugar and cheese mixture. Fold in the mini chocolate chips and store in the refrigerator until ready to use, but not longer than 24 hours. Fill the cannoli shells about 2 hours before serving, but not before as the shells may get soggy if filled longer than a few hours. Enjoy!

Mini flour tortillas make great homemade cannoli shells. Simply wrap around a cannoli mold and fry lightly in oil in fry pan or skillet for 1-2 minutes on each side. Remove from heat and drain on paper towels.

Asteroid Belt Rock Candy

The Asteroid Belt lies between Mars and Jupiter and consists of over 40,000 asteroids. Recipe from 6th grade Science Class.

Ingredients

- ▶ 5 Cups Granulated Sugar
- ▶ 3½ Cups Boiling Water

Equipment

- ◆ 1 Wooden Spoon or Tablespoon
- ◆ 1 Quart Glass Jar
- ◆ 1 Metal Washer or large Paper Clip
- ◆ 1 Piece of String or Twine 8 inches long
- ◆ 1 Pencil

Directions

Pour water in pan and bring to a boil. Add the sugar one cup at a time until all the sugar is dissolved. Pour mixture into the glass jar. Tie a metal washer or paper clip to one end of the string and tie the other end around the pencil. Place the pencil across the top of the jar and roll the string around the pencil until the metal washer or paper clip is almost touching the bottom of the jar. Place the jar in a warm place for 5-7 days. Crystals should start growing on the string. As the water and sugar mixture evaporates from the jar more crystals will form. Remove string with crystals from jar. Crystals are edible if desired. It is best not to let crystals form for more than two weeks.

Jupiter Red Spot Jell-O Shots

Fifth and largest planet from the Sun Jupiter is named for the Roman god of sky and thunder. It is a gas giant with a famous large Red Spot formed by violent storms. These Jell-O Shots are great on a warm summer day, and fun to make with kids.

Ingredients

▶ 1 3 Ounce Package of Cherry or Strawberry Jell-O

▶ 1 Cup Water

▶ 1 small jar of Maraschino Cherries

Directions

Follow directions on Jell-O package for preparation, adding boiling and cold water to the dry Jell-O mix until completely dissolved. Pour the mixture into small plastic, glass or paper cups. Cut maraschino cherries into small pieces and place a cherry piece into each plastic, glass or paper cup. Refrigerate for 4-6 hours until the Jell-O shots set and enjoy. *Servings: About 15-18 Jupiter Jell-O Shots.*

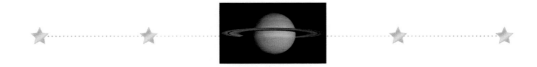

Saturn Stew

Saturn is the 6th planet from the Sun. It is a gas giant with beautiful rings composed of ice and rock with over 60 moons. Saturn is named for the Roman god of Agriculture Saturnus.

Ingredients

- ▶ 2 Pounds Potatoes, peeled and cubed
- ▶ 2 Pounds Boneless Beef or Chuck roast
- ▶ 4 Carrots, chopped or diced
- ▶ 1 Onion, chopped
- ▶ 1 Celery Stalk, chopped
- ▶ 1 Cup frozen Cut corn, thawed
- ▶ 1 Cup frozen Green Beans, thawed
- ▶ 3 Tablespoons Flour
- ▶ ¾ Cup Beef Broth
- ▶ ⅓ Cup Green or Black Olives, diced

Directions

In a large pot or Dutch oven, mix potatoes, carrots, onion and celery. Cut boneless beef meat or chuck roast into small pieces, then sear the meat pieces in a fry pan. Let cool, then coat the meat pieces with flour evenly. Add meat pieces to the pot. Top mixture with beef broth, adding salt and pepper to taste. Cover and cook on low heat for about 60-75 minutes, or until meat is tender. Stir mixture a few times while cooking. Add corn, green beans, and olives, cooking an additional 25-35 minutes. *Servings: 8-10 bowls of stew.*

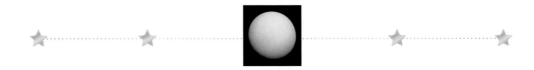

Uranus Ultimate Barbeque Sauce

Seventh planet from the Sun, Uranus was discovered by Astronomer William Herschel in 1781 and named for the Greek god Ouranos, father of the Sky. Uranus is an icy gas giant with rings, blue green in color, with an axis severely tilted to the Sun.

Ingredients

- ▶ 1 Clove Garlic, minced
- ▶ 1 Tablespoon Worcestershire Sauce
- ▶ 1 Teaspoon Dijon Mustard
- ▶ 4 Ounces Tomato Sauce
- ▶ ½ Cup White Wine Vinegar
- ▶ ¼ Cup Honey
- ▶ ¼ Cup Lemon Juice
- ▶ ¼ Cup Molasses
- ▶ ⅓ Cup Brown Sugar
- ▶ ¼ Cup Water
- ▶ ½ Teaspoon Salt
- ▶ ⅛ Teaspoon Cayenne Pepper (optional)
- ▶ ⅛ Teaspoon Black Pepper

Directions

Mix ingredients in saucepan. Bring to a boil, then simmer for 25 minutes or until sauce thickens. Enjoy with your favorite dishes. Makes about 1 cup of Barbeque sauce.

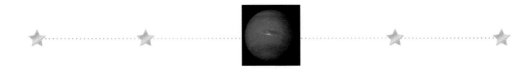

Neptune Noodles

Eighth planet from the Sun Neptune is an icy gas giant named for the Roman god of the Sea. Blue in color with six rings, surrounded by fourteen moons it is also the coldest planet in the Solar System. Winds as high as 1500 miles per hour have been recorded on Neptune.

Ingredients

- ▶ 1 Package Chicken or Vegetable Ramen Noodles
- ▶ 1 Medium Tomato or 3 Roma tomatoes, chopped
- ▶ 1 Cup Cheddar Cheese, grated or shredded
- ▶ ½ Pound Smoked Salmon or Tuna, cut into pieces
- ▶ ½ Cup Onion, chopped (optional)
- ▶ 2 Tablespoons Ranch Dressing (optional)

Directions

Cook noodles according to directions on package and drain. Mix ⅓ of noodle seasoning packet into the noodles. Mix other ingredients together in a bowl and fold into the noodles. Add dressing if desired. *Servings: 2-3 bowls of Neptune noodles.*

Pluto Pizza Puffs

Pluto, now labeled a "dwarf" planet as of 2006, was discovered by American Astronomer Clyde Tombaugh at Lowell Observatory in Flagstaff, Arizona on February 18, 1930. Pluto is named for the Roman god of the Underworld and is smaller than Earth's moon.

Ingredients

- ▶ 2 Cups Cheddar Cheese, grated
- ▶ 2 Cans Refrigerated Buttermilk Biscuits
- ▶ Olive or Vegetable Oil
- ▶ 1 Jar Meat flavored or Marinara Pasta Sauce
- ▶ ⅓ Cup Pepperoni or Salami, chopped

Equipment

- ◆ Tongs

Directions

Mix cheese and pepperoni together. Open biscuit containers and roll each biscuit into a circle. Spread a small amount of pasta sauce in the center of each biscuit, then add cheese and pepperoni filling to the center, fold in half and pinch edges together firmly. Using tongs cook in large fry pan or skillet brushed with olive or vegetable oil until biscuits brown on one side. Turn over and cook until brown on other side, then remove from fry pan or skillet and brush lightly with oil. Serve warm. *Servings: About 15-16 Pluto Pizza Puffs.*

Charon Cucumber Salad

Charon is the largest of five moons circling Pluto.

Ingredients

- ▶ 2-3 Cucumbers, sliced
- ▶ 1 Onion, cut into rings or chopped
- ▶ ½ Cup White or Red Wine Vinegar
- ▶ ½ Cup Sugar
- ▶ Celery or Sesame Seeds (optional)
- ▶ Salt
- ▶ Pepper

Directions

Add onion rings to sliced cucumbers. Mix vinegar and sugar together and pour over cucumbers. Sprinkle with salt, pepper, celery or sesame seeds (optional). Chill or serve. Refrigerate any left over. *Servings: 3-4 salad bowls.*

Great Galaxies, Constellations and Comets...

Milky Way Heavenly Hash

The Milky Way is a beautiful barred spiral galaxy, about 100,000 light years across containing over 200 billion stars and our home Earth in the Solar System.

Ingredients

- ▶ 8 Ounce Container Cool Whip, thawed
- ▶ 1 20 Ounce can crushed pineapple
- ▶ 1 3 Ounce package Instant Pistachio Pudding Mix
- ▶ 1 Jar Maraschino Cherries, chopped (optional)
- ▶ 1 Cup almonds or walnuts, chopped
- ▶ 1 Cup Miniature Marshmellows

Directions

Mix all ingredients in a large bowl and chill for 2-3 hours. Serve. *Servings: About 5-6 dessert size servings.*

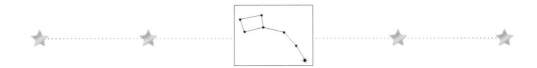

North Star Poles

Polaris, also known as the North Star or "Pole" Star is the star at the end of the Little Dipper's handle in the Constellation of Ursa Minor – the "Little Bear". Stars in the northern hemisphere appear to rotate around it.

Ingredients

- ▶ 1 Bag Chocolate Chips
- ▶ 1 Bag Large Pretzel Sticks or Rods
- ▶ 1 Jar Colored Sprinkles

Equipment

- ◆ Wax Paper or Aluminum Foil Sheets

Directions

Melt chocolate chips in a pan over low heat. Dip each pretzel stick into the melted chocolate covering about one third of the pretzel stick. Remove from heat and roll the chocolate covered part of the pretzel stick in the colored sprinkles. Place on wax paper or aluminum foil sheets and let cool. *Servings: About 24 North Star Poles.*

Orion Omelettes

The Constellation Orion, the "Hunter" in Greek mythology, is well known in northern skies. Orion's three "Belt" stars are prominent in the night sky as are supergiants Rigel and Betelgeuse, the two brightest stars in the Constellation.

Ingredients

- ▶ 2 Eggs
- ▶ 2 Teaspoons Butter or Margarine
- ▶ ¼ Cup Cheddar Cheese, shredded
- ▶ ¼ Cup Black or Green Olives
- ▶ ¼ Cup Tomatoes, diced
- ▶ ¼ Cup Bacon or Sausage, cooked
- ▶ Salt
- ▶ Pepper

Directions

Beat egg yolks and whites in a bowl until well blended. Cut cooked bacon or sausage into small pieces. Heat butter in a skillet or fry pan and pour eggs into skillet or pan, covering the bottom. When eggs are browned slightly on the bottom, add cheese, tomatoes, bacon and olives to the eggs, cook for 1-2 minutes longer, then fold the egg mixture in half with a spatula or fry pan flipper and cook another 1-2 minutes. Add salt and pepper to taste. *Servings: 1-2 omelettes.*

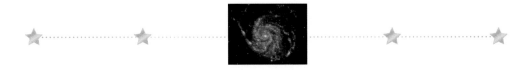

Pinwheel Galaxy Swirls

The Pinwheel is a spiral galaxy in the Constellation of Ursa Major – the "Great Bear". The Hubble Space Telescope captured stunning photographs of the Pinwheel in 2006.

Ingredients

- ▶ 3 Cups Flour
- ▶ 1½ Cups Unsalted Butter
- ▶ 1 Cup Confectioner's Sugar
- ▶ ⅔ Cup Granulated Sugar
- ▶ ¼ Cup Cocoa Powder
- ▶ 1 Tablespoon Vanilla or Almond Extract
- ▶ 1 Teaspoon Salt
- ▶ 1 Teaspoon Baking Powder

Equipment

- ◆ Aluminum Foil Plastic Wrap

Directions

Place butter, confectioner's and granulated sugar in a bowl and cream until fully blended. In another bowl mix the flour, salt and baking powder. Add the two mixtures and blend until a dough forms. Break the dough in half and add the cocoa mix to one half of the dough. Mix well. Wrap each dough mixture in foil or plastic wrap and place in refrigerator for 2 hours. Remove refrigerated dough and roll out each mixture. Put the dough with the cocoa on top of the one without cocoa and roll together creating a swirl. Cut ¼ inch rounds and place 2 inches apart on ungreased cookie sheet. Bake at 350 degrees Fahrenheit for 14-15 minutes. *Servings: About 3 dozen Pinwheel Swirls.*

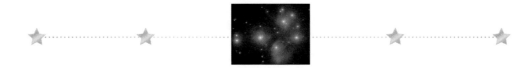

Pleiades Pumpkin Pancakes

Pleiades, a cluster of 7 stars called the "Seven Sisters" in Greek mythology, has only six stars visible at one time, the seventh "lost" or invisible. The Pleiades star cluster can be seen from most any point on Earth's surface.

Ingredients

- ▶ 2 Cups Flour
- ▶ 1¾ Cups Milk
- ▶ 1 Egg
- ▶ 2 Tablespoons Vegetable Oil
- ▶ 2 Tablespoons Brown Sugar
- ▶ 1 Tablespoon Baking Powder
- ▶ 2 Teaspoons Pumpkin Spice
- ▶ 1 Teaspoon Salt
- ▶ ½ Teaspoon Cinnamon
- ▶ ⅛ Teaspoon Ground Nutmeg

Directions

Mix all dry ingredients together in a bowl. In a separate bowl mix milk, egg and oil until well blended. Slowly add the dry ingredients to the milk, egg and oil mixture. Prepare pan, skillet or griddle for pancakes and brush with oil. Pour batter into pan, skillet or griddle slowly making pancakes about 7-8 inches around. Cook until bubbles on top of pancakes break. Flip pancakes and cook for about 1-2 minutes longer. Remove from heat and serve with syrup of your choice. *Servings: About 7-8 pancakes.*

Sombrero Salsa

The Sombrero is an unusual looking galaxy found in the Constellation of Virgo. The large white bulge at its center along with a broad rim of dust resembles the Mexican hat the sombrero. The Sombrero galaxy has a massive black hole at its center.

Ingredients

- ▶ 2 Pounds Cherry tomatoes, chopped
- ▶ 1 Red Bell Pepper, diced
- ▶ 1 Green Bell Pepper, diced
- ▶ 1 Bunch Fresh Cilantro, chopped
- ▶ 1 Large Onion, diced
- ▶ ¾ Cup Lime Juice
- ▶ ¼ Cup Olive Oil
- ▶ 2 Tablespoons Salt
- ▶ 1½ Tablespoons Chili Powder

Directions

Combine all the chopped and diced ingredients with the olive oil, lime juice, chili powder and salt in a bowl. Serve and refrigerate any left over salsa. *Servings: 1 large bowl of salsa.*

Southern Cross Cheese Straws

The Southern Cross Constellation is the most prominent celestial object in the southern skies. It has been used in navigation since ancient times and is part of the Australian flag as well as many other flags of southern hemisphere countries.

Ingredients

- ▶ 2 Cups Grated Cheddar Cheese
- ▶ 1¼ Cups Flour
- ▶ ½ Cup Butter
- ▶ ¼ Teaspoon Salt
- ▶ ⅛ Teaspoon Red Pepper (optional)

Directions

Mix all ingredients together well in a bowl. Roll mixture, then cut into 4-5 inch strips. Place strips on nonstick baking sheet and bake in oven at 350 degrees Fahrenheit for 15 minutes or until strips are golden brown. Remove and cool. *Servings: About 18-24 cheese straws.*

Andromeda Applesauce

The Andromeda Galaxy is the Milky Way Galaxy's nearest neighbor. A beautiful spiral galaxy in the northern sky Andromeda is estimated to have over 1 trillion stars.

Ingredients

- ▶ 6-7 Honey Crisp or Red Apples
- ▶ 1 Cup Water
- ▶ ¼ Cup Sugar
- ▶ ¾ Tablespoon Ground Cinnamon

Equipment

- ◆ Strainer

Directions

Peel and core the apples. Cut into strips. Place apples in saucepan, adding water, sugar, and ground cinnamon. Simmer until apples are soft, then mash until smooth in texture. At this point the mixture can be strained if desired. Cool and serve. *Servings: 2-3 bowls of applesauce.*

Cassiopeia Cupcakes

Constellation Cassiopeia in the northern skies is named after a vain Greek queen Cassiopeia. It forms a "W" opposite Constellation Ursa Major – the "Great Bear".

Ingredients

- ▶ 2 Cups Flour
- ▶ 1 Cup Sugar
- ▶ 1 Cup Butter, softened
- ▶ 2 Eggs, yolks separated from whites
- ▶ ½ Cup Orange Juice
- ▶ 1 Teaspoon Vanilla Extract
- ▶ 1½ Teaspoons Baking Powder
- ▶ ½ Teaspoon Salt

Equipment

- ◆ Cupcake Liners Muffin Tins Hand Mixer

Directions

Combine butter, sugar, egg yolks and vanilla in a bowl, mixing well. Mix flour, salt and baking soda in a separate bowl. Add the bowl's ingredients to the first bowl while also adding the orange juice slowly. Beat egg whites with electric hand mixer until stiff and fold in egg whites. Fill cupcake liners ⅔ full with batter. Preheat oven to 350 degrees Fahrenheit and bake for 15-17 minutes or until a toothpick inserted in the center of cupcakes removes cleanly. Cool cupcakes completely before frosting with a frosting of your choice. *Servings: About 24 cupcakes.*

Comet Tail Soup

Comets are traveling objects in the Solar System with a nucleus of ice and dusty rocks sometimes looking like a "dirty snowball" with a long tail. Comet Halley is one of the most famous comets, known to ancient astronomers as early as 240 B.C.E.

Ingredients

- ▶ 6 Cups Water
- ▶ 1 Cup Milk, heated
- ▶ 2 Carrots, peeled and sliced
- ▶ 2 Potatoes, peeled and sliced
- ▶ 2 Onions
- ▶ 1 Cup Celery, washed and chopped
- ▶ 1 Cup Shell Pasta of your choice
- ▶ 1 Tablespoon Butter or Margarine
- ▶ ½ Cube Beef or Chicken Buillon Cube

Directions

Place all ingredients in a soup pot or other large pot. Cover and let boil over medium heat for 25-30 minutes. Salt and pepper to taste and serve with bread of your choice. *Servings: 8-10 soup bowl servings.*

Crab Cakes

The Crab Nebula is a left over remnant from an exploding star observed in 1054 A.D. by Chinese astronomers. British Astronomer John Bevis located the remnant in 1731, and British Astronomer William Parsons sketched it in 1844 thinking it resembled a crab.

Ingredients

- ▶ 1 Pound Crabmeat
- ▶ 1 Egg, beaten
- ▶ 1 Clove Garlic, ground or minced
- ▶ ¼ Cup Cracker or Bread Crumbs
- ▶ 2 Tablespoons Mayonnaise
- ▶ 2 Teaspoons Butter
- ▶ 1 Teaspoon Worcestershire Sauce

Directions

Mix all ingredients together in a bowl and form into small cakes. Saute crab cakes in butter until browned on each side. Serve hot. *Servings: 10-12 crab cakes.*

Big Dipper Dip

The Big Dipper is located in part of the Constellation Ursa Major – the "Great Bear" and is one of the most recognizable sky objects in the northern hemisphere.

Ingredients

- ▶ 8 Ounces Cream Cheese
- ▶ 1 Cup Bacon bits or cooked bacon, diced
- ▶ ½ Cup Sour Cream
- ▶ 3 Tablespoons Horseradish
- ▶ 1 Tablespoon Parsley

Directions

Mix cream cheese and sour cream together in a bowl. Add other ingredients and refrigerate. Serve with favorite crackers or vegetables. *Servings: One medium bowl of dip.*

Great Astronomers and Observatories...

Astrolabe Avocado Dip

An astrolabe is an ancient instrument used by astronomers to study the position of stars and celestial objects. It is thought to have been created around the time of Greek Astronomer Ptolemy (ca 90 – 168 C.E.) or earlier.

Ingredients

- ▶ 1-2 Ripe Avocados
- ▶ 1 Clove of Garlic, peeled and chopped
- ▶ 1 Tablespoon Lemon Juice
- ▶ 1 Tablespoon Lime Juice
- ▶ ½ Teaspoon Salt
- ▶ ½ Teaspoon Pepper
- ▶ ¼ Teaspoon Ground Chili Pepper

Directions

Cut avocado(s) in half and remove pit(s). Scoop out the flesh of the avocado(s) and mix with the other ingredients in a bowl. Blend well and serve. *Servings: 1 small bowl of avocado dip.*

Brahe Baked Beans

Tycho Brahe (1546-1601) was a Danish Astronomer known for the accuracy of his work on the Solar System and fixed star observations before the invention of the telescope.

Ingredients

- ▶ 6 Slices of Bacon, cut into small pieces
- ▶ 1 Large Bermuda onion
- ▶ 1 Can (16 ounce) Baked Beans
- ▶ 1 Can (16 ounce) Butter Beans, drained
- ▶ 8 Ounces Water
- ▶ 2 Tablespoons Brown Sugar
- ▶ 1 Tablespoon Dark Molasses
- ▶ ½ Cup Tomato Paste, thinned
- ▶ ¼ Cup Dijon Mustard
- ▶ ¼ Cup Worcestershire Sauce

Directions

Preheat oven to 350 degrees Fahrenheit. Chop onion and place with bacon in a fry pan. Cook until bacon and onion are browned. Mix with other ingredients and pour into a 2 or 3 quart casserole dish and bake for 1 hour uncovered. *Servings: About 10-15 individual servings.*

Cerro Tololo Chili

Cerro Tololo Inter-American Observatory (CTIO) located in Chile, South America, is home to the "Blanco" Telescope and others in the southern hemisphere. "Blanco" came about through an agreement signed by Presidents Lyndon Johnson and Eduardo Frei in 1967.

Ingredients

- ▶ 2 Cups Chicken or Turkey breast, cooked, diced
- ▶ 1½ Cups Chicken or Vegetable Broth
- ▶ 1 16 Ounce Jar Salsa Verde
- ▶ 1 14 Ounce Can Great Northern Beans (optional)
- ▶ 1 Onion, diced
- ▶ 1 Tablespoon Vegetable or Canola Oil
- ▶ Salt
- ▶ Pepper

Directions

Dice cooked chicken or turkey. Saute onion and oil for 5-6 minutes in a medium size pan. Add beans, chicken or vegetable broth and salsa verde to onion and oil mixture. Bring mixture to a boil, stirring a few times, then reduce heat to medium. Simmer for 12-15 minutes, then add the diced chicken or turkey breast pieces. Salt and pepper to taste. Serve with crackers or bread of your choice. *Servings: Makes about 5-6 bowls of chili.*

Copernicus Caramels

Nicolaus Copernicus (1473-1543) was a Polish Astronomer who introduced a new theory about the Solar System orbiting the Sun, not the Earth, a radical concept at the time.

Ingredients

- ▶ 2 Cups Granulated Sugar
- ▶ 2 Cups Light Corn Syrup
- ▶ 1 Cup Cream or Half and Half
- ▶ 1½ Stick Butter, softened
- ▶ ⅔ Cup Orange Juice Concentrate, thawed
- ▶ ⅛ Teaspoon Salt

Equipment

- ◆ Sheets of Aluminum Foil
- ◆ 8 inch square pan
- ◆ Candy Thermometer
- ◆ Non stick cooking spray
- ◆ Non stick cooking spray
- ◆ Sheets of Wax Paper

Directions

Line an 8 inch pan with aluminum foil and spray with non stick cooking spray. In a saucepan combine sugar, salt, corn syrup and orange juice concentrate. Bring to a boil, stirring frequently. When the mixture starts to boil insert the candy thermometer and cook until the thermometer reaches 280 degrees Fahrenheit, stirring occasionally. Add cream or Half and Half along with softened butter and continue cooking until thermometer reaches 245 degrees Fahrenheit. Remove from heat and pour caramels into the lined pan and leave overnight. The next day cut caramels into small pieces and wrap individually in wax paper. *Servings: 25-30 Copernicus Caramels.*

Fleming French Toast

Williamina Fleming (1857-1911) was a Scottish-American Astronomer who invented a system of classification for stars and cataloguing them. She is credited with the discovery of the Horsehead Nebula in 1888 and the first white dwarf stars in 1910.

Ingredients

▶ 2 Eggs

▶ 4 Slices of Bread

▶ ¾ Cup Milk

▶ 1 Tablespoon Butter

▶ 1 Teaspoon Vanilla Extract

▶ Cinnamon

▶ Sugar

▶ Syrup of your choice

Directions

Melt butter in pan. Mix eggs, milk and vanilla extract in bowl until well blended. Dip slices of bread in mixture until thoroughly covered. Brown one side of the soaked bread slices in pan, then turn over the slices and brown other side. Remove from pan and sprinkle with sugar and cinnamon. Serve with syrup of your choice. *Servings: 1-2 individual servings.*

Galileo Gumdrops

Galileo Galilei (1564-1642) was a famous Italian Astronomer and Mathematician. He discovered many objects in the Solar System, among them moons around Jupiter, mountains and craters on Earth's moon, the phases of Venus and sunspots.

Ingredients

▶ 1 Cup Sugar

▶ 1 Cup Light Corn Syrup

▶ ¾ Cup Orange Juice

▶ 1¾ Ounce Package Powdered Fruit Pectin

▶ ½ Teaspoon Baking Soda

▶ 2 Drops Yellow Food Coloring

▶ 2 Drops Red Food Coloring

Equipment

◆ Candy Thermometer

◆ Sheets of Aluminum Foil

◆ Wooden Spoon

◆ 9 x 5 inch loaf pan

Directions

Line 9 x 5 inch loaf pan with aluminum foil and brush with oil. Combine sugar and corn syrup in a 2 quart saucepan. Bring mixture to a boil over medium heat until sugar dissolves. Insert the candy thermometer into the mixture and continue cooking until it reaches 280 degrees Fahrenheit. In another saucepan combine orange juice, pectin and baking soda. Bring to a boil over high heat, stirring constantly. After boiling, reduce heat to low and slowly pour the sugar mixture into the orange juice mixture, stirring constantly with wooden spoon. Remove from heat, add the food coloring and stir. Pour gumdrops into loaf pan and let stand overnight. The next day remove the foil, cut the gumdrops into 1 inch squares and roll in sugar. Enjoy. *Servings: 25-30 gumdrops.*

Gandolfo Grenadines

The Vatican Observatory Headquarters are located at Castel Gandolfo, Italy. It is one of the oldest Observatories in the world with works by famous astronomers Galileo, Copernicus, Newton and Kepler housed in its library.

Ingredients

- ▶ 1 Cup Frozen Lime Juice
- ▶ 2 Cups Ginger Ale, Sprite or 7-Up (Regular or Diet)
- ▶ 6 Tablespoons Grenadine Syrup

Equipment

- ♦ Blender

Directions

Add frozen lime juice, Ginger Ale, Sprite or 7-Up, and grenadine to blender. Blend mix for 1 minute. Pour into glasses of your choice and enjoy. *Servings: 5-6 Eight ounce glasses.*

Greenwich Greens

The Royal Observatory, located in Greenwich, United Kingdom, is a site founded in the late 1600s for celestial research. The Prime Meridian passes through the Observatory and is site 000 for Greenwich Mean Time (GMT).

Ingredients

▶ 1 Head of Butter Lettuce, chopped

▶ ½ Bunch of Radishes, sliced or diced

▶ 2 Tablespoons Olive Oil

▶ 1¾ Tablespoons Red Wine Vinegar

▶ Salt

▶ Pepper

Directions

Combine lettuce and radishes in a large bowl. Mix in red wine vinegar and olive oil, then toss. Salt and pepper to taste. *Servings: 3-4 salad bowls of greens.*

Griffith Grahams

Griffith Observatory, opened in 1935 in Los Angeles, California, is one of the most visited Observatories in the world. The site was donated by philanthropist Griffith J. Griffith with his desire that the Observatory and exhibits be freely accessible to the public.

Ingredients

- ▶ 1½ Cups Milk
- ▶ ½ Cup Creamy Peanut Butter
- ▶ 1 Package Instant Chocolate Pudding Mix
- ▶ 1-2 Boxes of Graham Crackers

Directions

Mix milk, creamy peanut butter and instant chocolate pudding mix together. Spread mixture between two graham crackers and enjoy. Store extras in refrigerator or freezer. *Servings: Makes about 2-3 dozen Griffith Grahams.*

Hale Hearty Apple Cider

George Ellery Hale (1868-1938) was an American Astronomer who specialized in studying sunspots and solar activity. He was instrumental in the building of telescopes at Yerkes, Mt. Wilson and Palomar Observatories.

Ingredients

- ▶ 1 Gallon Apple Cider or Apple Juice
- ▶ ⅓ Cup Brown Sugar, packed down
- ▶ ¼ Cup Butter, softened
- ▶ ¼ Cup Honey
- ▶ ¼ Teaspoon Ground Cinnamon
- ▶ ¼ Teaspoon Ground Nutmeg
- ▶ Cinnamon or Peppermint Sticks (optional)

Directions

Mix brown sugar, butter, honey, cinnamon and nutmeg until well blended. Heat apple cider or juice in pan, then pour into cups or mugs and add 1 tablespoon butter mixture per cup or mug. Add cinnamon or peppermint sticks if desired. Enjoy. *Servings: 8-10 Eight ounce glasses or mugs of apple cider.*

Herschel Herb Brushetta

British Astronomer William Herschel (1738-1802) is credited with discovering planet Uranus in 1781. He was an early user of prisms in the field of spectrophotometry.

Ingredients

- ▶ 1½ Pounds Plum or Cherry Tomatoes, chopped
- ▶ ⅓ Cup Fresh Basil Leaves, chopped
- ▶ 1 Tablespoon Oregano Leaves, chopped
- ▶ 1 Tablespoon Basalmic Vinegar
- ▶ 1 Tablespoon Olive Oil
- ▶ 1 Teaspoon Garlic, minced
- ▶ 1 Teaspoon Lemon Juice
- ▶ Salt
- ▶ Pepper
- ▶ 6 Slices of bread with crust or toast

Directions

Mix tomatoes, herbs, oil and lemon juice in a bowl, adding salt and pepper to taste. Spoon the mix onto slices of crusty bread or toast and enjoy. *Servings: 3-6 slices.*

Hubble Hot Chocolate

Edwin Hubble (1889-1953) was an American Astronomer and leading cosmologist of the 20th Century. His research and scientific studies showed that the Universe is expanding. In 1983 the Hubble Space Telescope (HST) was named for Edwin Hubble.

Ingredients

- ▶ 3 Ounces of unsweetened chocolate
- ▶ 2 Squares of sweetened chocolate
- ▶ 4 Cups Milk
- ▶ ¾ Cup Brown Sugar
- ▶ ⅓ Cup Water
- ▶ ⅛ Teaspoon Salt

Directions

Melt the unsweetened chocolate, chocolate squares and water together in a pan. Heat 4 cups of milk in another saucepan, then add the chocolate and water mixture along with the brown sugar and salt to the milk. Stir until smooth texture. Pour into individual cups or mugs, add whipped cream or marshmellows if desired. Enjoy! *Servings: 4-5 Eight ounce cups or mugs.*

Kitt Peak Potato Squares

Kitt Peak National Observatory is located near Tucson, Arizona. It has a large array of optical telescopes, including the world's largest solar telescope, along with two radio telescopes. The Observatory is famous for original research into asteroids.

Ingredients

- ▶ 6 Potatoes
- ▶ ½ Cup onions, chopped
- ▶ ½ Tablespoon Olive Oil
- ▶ ½ Teaspoon Salt
- ▶ ¼ Teaspoon Pepper

Directions

Bring a pan of water to boiling temperature on stove. Place potatoes in pan and cook, with skins, for 20 minutes. Remove from water, remove skins and lightly shred potatoes. Mix potatoes with onions, salt and pepper. Shape potatoes into 3-4 inch squares. Heat oil in fry pan and add potato squares. Cook over medium heat until potato squares are brown on one side, then turn potato squares over and cook until brown and crunchy on other side. Remove from stove and drain on paper towels. *Servings: 8-10 Potato Squares.*

Mauna Kea Koolers

Mauna Kea, Hawaii is home to several optical and infrared telescopes, including the twin W.M. Keck Observatory Keck 1 and 2 telescopes, once considered the largest in the world. Each Keck telescope primary mirror is composed of 36 hexagonal segments.

Ingredients

▶ 8 Ounces Pineapple Juice

▶ 8 Ounces Frozen Orange Juice

▶ Juice from ½ Lemon or Lime

Equipment

◆ Blender

Directions

Mix ingredients in blender until smooth, about 1-2 minutes. Pour into glasses and enjoy! *Servings: Makes about 4 Six ounce koolers.*

Messier Meatballs

Charles Messier (1730-1817) was a French Astronomer who searched for comets and created the famous Messier catalog of deep sky celestial objects. Originally the catalog contained 103 objects. Seven additional objects were added in the 20th Century.

Ingredients

- ▶ 1 Pound Ground Beef or Turkey
- ▶ 1 Egg
- ▶ 1 Teaspoon Worcestershire Sauce
- ▶ ¼ Cup Onion, chopped
- ▶ ¼ Cup Milk
- ▶ ⅓ Cup Bread Crumbs
- ▶ ¾ Teaspoon Salt
- ▶ ¼ Teaspoon Pepper

Equipment

- ◆ 9 x 13 inch baking pan

Directions

Mix all ingredients in a bowl. Shape into 1½ inch balls and place in a lightly greased 9 x 13 inch baking pan. Bake uncovered at 375 degrees Fahrenheit for 25 to 30 minutes. Drain fat from pan after removing from oven. *Servings: About 18 Messier meatballs.*

Mt. Wilson Haystacks

Mt. Wilson Observatory is home to the 100 inch Hooker Telescope, once considered the world's largest telescope until the 200 inch Hale Telescope opened on Mt. Palomar in 1948.

Ingredients

▶ 1 Cup Semi Sweet Chocolate Chips
▶ ½ Cup Peanut Butter
▶ ½ Cup Slivered Almond Pieces (optional)
▶ 2 Tablespoons Butter or Margarine
▶ 2 Cups Chow Mein Noodles

Equipment

◆ Sheets of Wax Paper

Directions

Mix chocolate chips and peanut butter in a large pan over a safe heat source, such as a Coleman stove, barbeque grill outside, or on a stove inside, until melted. Stir almonds (optional) and chow mein noodles into chocolate chip/peanut butter mixture, stirring thoroughly and chow mein noodles are completely covered. Drop by tablespoonfuls onto wax paper sheets and let cool for 45 minutes and enjoy. *Servings: About 15 Mt. Wilson Haystacks.*

Palomar Potato Puffs

The 200 inch Hale Telescope is located in the Palomar Mountain Range in San Diego County, California. The reflecting telescope is named after Astronomer George Ellery Hale and was considered the largest telescope in the world from 1949-1975.

Ingredients

- ▶ 2 Eggs
- ▶ 2 Cups Mashed Potatoes
- ▶ 1 Tablespoon Grated Cheddar Cheese
- ▶ 1 Tablespoon Chives
- ▶ 1 Teaspoon Dried Minced Onion
- ▶ 2-3 Tablespoons Melted Butter or Margarine

Equipment

- ◆ Blender Paper Muffin Cups Muffin Tin

Directions

Place 6 medium potatoes in boiling water and cook until tender. Separate egg yolks from egg whites. Mix egg yolks with potatoes, cheddar cheese, chives and minced onion. Beat egg whites with blender until egg whites stiffen then add into the potato mixture. Place muffin cups into muffin tins on ungreased baking sheet. Brush muffin cups with melted butter and spoon potato mixture into muffin cups. Brush remaining butter over potatoes and bake at 375 degrees Fahrenheit for about 35 minutes or until lightly browned. *Servings: 12 Potato Puffs.*

Radio Radishes

Not all telescopes are optical. Some use radio waves such as the Very Large Array (VLA) at the National Radio Astronomy Observatory near Socorro, New Mexico to study the Universe. The VLA has the largest configuration of radio telescopes in the world.

Ingredients

- ▶ 5-6 Large Red Radishes
- ▶ 1 Tablespoon Honey
- ▶ 1 Bunch of Parsley (optional)
- ▶ ½ Tablespoon Butter or Margarine
- ▶ ⅓ Tablespoon Cinnamon

Directions

Clean radishes, chop or dice, then place in small casserole dish. Mix honey, butter or margarine and cinnamon in a small pan. Blend ingredients well and pour over the radishes. Bake about 30 minutes at 350 degrees Fahrenheit. Place radishes on small salad plates or bowls and add the parsley as garnish.

Servings: 5-6 small salad size plates or bowls.

Stonehedge Smoothies

Stonehedge is considered a possible prehistoric archeoastronomy site, located in Wiltshire, England. Large stones placed in concentric rings, some older than 5000 years, have alignments in the direction of the summer and winter solstices.

Ingredients

- ¾ Cup Lowfat Yogurt
- ½ Cup White Grape Juice
- ½ Cup Strawberries, fresh or thawed
- 1 Tablespoon Sugar
- 3-4 Ice cubes

Equipment

- Blender

Directions

Place ice cubes in blender then add other ingredients. Blend together for about 45 seconds or until smooth. Serve and enjoy. *Servings: 3-4 Six ounce glasses.*

Yerkes Yammies

Yerkes Observatory is located in Williams Bay, Wisconsin. It was founded by famed Astronomer George Ellery Hale in 1897 and has been the work site of many famous astronomers, including Edwin Hubble and "astronomer of the people" Carl Sagan.

Ingredients

- ▶ 1 Large Can of Yams, drained
- ▶ 2 Tablespoons Butter or Margarine
- ▶ 1 Tablespoon Olive Oil
- ▶ ¼ Cup Brown Sugar

Equipment

- ◆ 8 inch square baking pan

Directions

Mix yams, brown sugar, olive oil and butter or margarine in a large bowl until mixture is a lumpy texture. Place in an 8 inch square baking pan and bake at 400 degrees Fahrenheit for 35 minutes. Remove from oven, let cool for 10 minutes and serve. *Servings: 8-10 individual servings.*

A Special Space Shuttle Tribute...

Space Shuttle Scoodles

The historic Space Shuttle program, developed by NASA for reusable human spaceflight, flew 135 missions from 1981-2011, from the Kennedy Space Center in Florida.

Ingredients

▶ 2 Cups Flour

▶ 2 Cups Sugar

▶ 2 Eggs

▶ 1 Cup Softened Butter

▶ 4 Teaspoons Cinnamon

▶ 2 Teaspoons Cream of Tartar

▶ 1 Teaspoon Baking Soda

Equipment

♦ Hand Mixer

Directions

Preheat oven to 350 degrees Fahrenheit. Grease cookie sheets. Mix together cream of tartar, flour, baking soda in a bowl. In another bowl, using an electric hand mixer, cream butter and 1½ cups of sugar. Add eggs to the mixture and continue blending. Mix flour and cream of tartar mixture into butter mixture until smooth and form into 1 inch balls. Mix ¼ cup sugar and cinnamon together in a small bowl and roll individual balls in the mixture. Place balls about 3 inches apart on cookie sheets and bake 10-12 minutes or until cookies are brown around edges. Let cool and remove from cookie sheets. *Servings: Around 24-30 Space Shuttle Scoodles.*

Measurements, Conversions and General Comments...

All the recipes are meaured in American Standard units for volume and weight. Temperature degrees are in Fahrenheit, not Celsius. Volumes are in ounces, not milliliters. Most ovens vary in temperatures. Cooking and baking times for the recipes are approximate. See chart below for some common Metric conversions.

American Standard / Metric

American Standard	Metric
1 Teaspoon - 1/4 fluid ounce	5 milliliters
1 Tablespoon - 1/2 fluid ounce	15 milliliters
1/4 Cup - 2 fluid ounces	60 milliliters
1/3 Cup - 3 fluid ounces	80 milliliters
1/2 Cup - 4 fluid ounces	120 milliliters
2/3 Cup - 5 fluid ounces	160 milliliters
3/4 Cup - 6 fluid ounces	180 milliliters
1 Cup - 8 fluid ounces	250 milliliters

Dry ingredients

1/4 ounce	7 grams
1/2 ounce	15 grams
3/4 ounce	20 grams
1 ounce	30 grams
16 ounces - 1 pound	455 grams

Temperature

212 Degrees Fahrenheit (boiling)	100 Degrees Celsius
350 Degrees Fahrenheit	177 Degrees Celsius
375 Degrees Fahrenheit	191 Degrees Celsius
400 Degrees Fahrenheit	204 Degrees Celsius

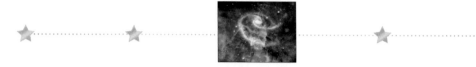

Notes

Notes

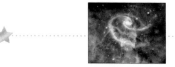

Image and Illustration Credits

All images associated with the final product of a recipe are attributed to the author Sherry A.Martinez

Thirteen NASA/JPL-Caltech images listed on pages 7,9,11,17,21,23,25,27,29,31,33,41,45 are in the Public Domain and do not imply an endorsement of any kind for any product, place or person by NASA/JPL-Caltech or their associated partners. More information on these images is available from the author if desired.

The following images and illustrations are credited to Sherry A. Martinez—Big Bang image Page 0, Moon Boot image page 15, Southern Cross Illustration page 47, Little Dipper Illustration, page 37, Cassiopeia Illustration, page 51, Astrolabe image, page 59, Mt. Wilson Illustration, page 88, Space Shuttle image, page 99

The following images are credited to Photographer Raul M. Martinez—Starbust image page 1, Sunspot images, page 3,and 5, Big Dipper image, page 57, Palomar Observatory image, page 91, Very Large Array image, page 93

Moon image Credit: Petr Kratpchvil—Public Domain License CC0 page 13

Milky Way image Credit: Mariam Espacio Goodfreephotos.com page 35

Griffith Observatory image Credit: pxhere.com. Public Domain License Creative Common Zero-CC0 page 75

Greenwich Observatory image Credit: Max Pixel. Creative Commons License 1.0 page 73

Kitt Peak Observatory image Credit: General Epitaph. Released into the Public Domain page 83

Mauna Kea Observatory image Credit: A. Woodcraft. Released into the Public Domain page 85

Yerkes Observatory image Credit: J. Takemann. Released into the Public Domain page 97

Fourteen images listed on pages 19,49,53,55,61,65,67,69,71,77,79,81,87,95 are in the Public Domain. More information on these images is available from the author if desired.

Made in the USA
San Bernardino,
CA